Asia U

A NIGHT WITH ME

Poems

A Night With Me
Poems

Written by Asia Upton

This is a work of creative nonfiction. Some parts have been fictionalized in varying degrees, for various purposes.

First edition

Cover and interior art by Asia Upton

ISBN 9780578335629

www.poetichumm.com

For those stuck in a waking nightmare,

Hoping for a different perspective to arrive like the rise of day.

Contents

A
NIGHT
WITH
ME

Part One:
After The Sun Sets
Breaking up with the day

I left my pride at the door
Kicked off my shoes
Glanced at my bills on the table
Wallowed a while in my blues
I took some pictures of my future
Shared some cocktails with my past

I said goodbye to the day
And hello to a darker path

A G A P E

It awaits inside the heart
Idle in uncharted depths
With no conditions

Ready to swallow whole
Fragmented and
Contoured
Views on
What i once believed
Love to be…

It lies at the center of
A chaste heart
That does beat
That does suffer
And is indeed
Intact

I don't believe hopeless romantics have broken hearts

TRANSITIONAL PLACE

The sun was going down
As was I
I turned on my lamp
And lit every candle

I tried to spark some light
Best I knew how

Darkness was creeping
The wind was
Rustling the leaves
I heard a voice
Call out to me
I answered hello?
Is anyone there?

The candles
Soon blown out
The room
Dark
Cold
Bare

H O L L O W

The   overflow   of   my   heart

Filled the   holes   inside yours

You   were   the   desert

And   I

The   ocean

You   want

So   desperately

To   suck   me   dry

Not   even   to   build   yourself

Only   to   break-even

My   heart   doesn't   know   how   to distinguish

I   always   had   the   fear

Of   feeling   empty   and   dead

But   I don't   know   how   to tell   my   heart

To   ride   shotgun…

When my   mind   never   took   drivers ed

FOOLISH THINGS I'VE DONE

I didn't know I was losing control
I raised up
Bent down
Rolled over
And sought out my flaws
Scoured the room for a comforting eye
Only to find shrewd gazes
Unearthing
Feelings inside of me
I've never felt before
I tried holding on
Chained myself to hell
Felt sorry
On repeat
Transformed
And cut myself in two
I removed all of me
And I added all of you

Fool

-ish

Things

I've

Done

WHOEVER *YOU* ARE

From *you*

I learned nothing

But

How to suffer

And play nice

Ruining my chances

Of success at getting it right

Asia Upton

PRICE OF A SOUL

You act like
It is an easy thing
Like it is special
To be used until empty
Thrown away without a thought
Left to
Rot

What amount of dignity
Would I have to give you
To satisfy your ego?
How much does it cost to please
The evil
That lies inside of you?

VIEWS

You were never looking at me

Or for me

And I

Was never looking at you

For you

Is there a difference?

FALSE HOPES

It's not your fault

That I'm not enough for you

Your fault is in

Making me believe I was

Why would you call it beautiful?

LOVE
NEVER
STAYS

How does your mind move so easily?
I'm burdened with confusion
Because I can't calculate
An accurate answer
I can't make full sentences out of love
I can't make sense of how it feels
In how it leaves

R E F L E C T

Everything I cross

I feel

Every sharp thing

Every smooth sail

It's real

BLACK GIRLS

Who is going to protect us?
Who will speak our name in love?
Who is going to honor our bodies?
These are things I wonder about
Worry about

Black girl
Who is special
But often misunderstood...
I don't think
I have an answer to these questions
I don't think
The world remembers who you are

What do we do
When we find ourselves puzzled
And confused?
We live in a blind world
Where strangers
Friends
Partners
And even family don't see us

The backs of our mothers
Carry the weight of worlds
And yet
They walk like nothing is holding them!

We are not storage for all the things
You don't want anymore
We are strong
But nobody
Should have to obtain this much strength

When will the world realize
That we hold, we give
Too much

DISCON NECT

I'm an artist

At times

I paint different realities

That don't exist

Such beautiful things

We could all imagine

Vision boards like

You've never seen

I find it hard to paint

Anything real for me

The colors don't

Look the same

NAKED TRUTHS

It ain't been easy
Revealing my true self

Without all the fixings
And the patches

But here I am
Leaking and scorn

Showing you
All the ways
I am open
All the ways
I am torn

EXPENSES

Woke and

Can't afford to dream

Life got to flow

By a symbiotic means

Fell in love with the sun

But now the day is done

And it is time to sleep

OPEN ROAD

Pain is not a roadblock

It's the gas in my tank

I'm ready for a good road trip

Don't plan on making a stop

Anytime soon

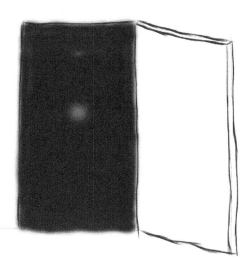

L I G H T N '   B U G S

I first beamed with him
Not knowing I already had the light inside me

He put me in his jar
Constricted in this glass
Little did he know
My glow
Would not last

And as time passed
He didn't need me...
So he freed me

Amongst the murky shadows, she radiated like a flare signaling for aid

CREATURES OF WANT

Sometimes

We are just

Needy little beings

Wanting others

To give us

What we can't give to ourselves

THE SINK

I'm growing tired with dreams of loving someone

I am bored with the hopes

Of it being beautiful

And good

How long can you ponder…

Things you've never had?

Feelings you never birthed?

Visions never touched?

I have fallen out of love with so many things

And now suddenly…I've fallen into myself

Part Two:
In The Heat Of The Night
Looking into the mirror

I am surrounded by darkness
And I am chasing God
I am seeking refuge in this storm
In the tunnel
I see the light
The thought of its embrace
Is what keeps me warm

T E R R O R I S T

I woke up inside a nightmare
The door was already closed
For me to exist in peace

I had to
Scrape
Dig
And teleport
My way into this world

I looked crazed
And unfit
I was a scare
And I was
Different

A myth come true

I was
The awakening
They were sleeping for

THE SONGS THEY PLAYED FOR ME

It was in their tone of voice
In the billboards that don't look like me
For all my life

I didn't want to be just nothing

But still
I followed its tune
I danced to the rhythm
It played on my blues

I KEEP TALKING MYSELF DOWN

I keep talking myself down
Off of that bridge
Thinking that I could fool myself
Into thinking something else
But I'm intrigued at
How it might sound
How I might crash
I want to know what it is like
To show what it is I've been feeling

NOCTURNAL

There were secrets
I wasn't good
I was a creature of the wild

I experienced love
In my pure heart
And destroyed it
In my savage ways

I planted some seeds of sunshine
Watered them with prayer
But I'm still here
Shifting through my emotions

Still here
Naked and bare
I haven't seen
The light of day
In years

Slept
But not rested

Calm
But not with peace

Silent
But screaming aches...

Aches in my body
That seep upward into
My breath
In
And out
Speaking a foreign language
With broken words

SHE WAS MEEK

She knew the ins
And a few of the outs
But her knowledge did her no good
She was courageous
Had a lot to say
Passionate but soft-spoken
The world could not hear her words
Her frustrations grew
And in time
She changed into someone new
Glancing into the mirror

She didn't recognize
Herself as well
She had
Bitten off her tongue
So she would not have
Such a complex
Story to tell
And
To tell it to so many
Who still
Would choose to
Misunderstand…
Her new
Native
Tongue
Is anger
And self-neglect

SINKHOLE

I didn't think about the how
Or the when
All I have is the desire…
To cut it off
Like a switch
    I want to fall into death
    The way that I fall asleep
My body acts against me
My thoughts fight me
All day
    I'm struggling
        How much will encouragement
        Do for me?
I am
Unmotivated
    Unmoved
Exhausted…no energy
    And confused
I am stuck
    And I know that I have to do all of this work
I am stuck
    And I'm not sure how I even got here
I think
    I was born a mistake
I think
    I was born in a sinkhole
And now I have to figure a way out
    Against destiny
Destiny…
    I'm fighting a battle
    I don't think I'm meant to win
And that makes me want to give in

SKIP THIS ONE

Last night I passed out

And

In the morning I woke up an hour late for work

I

Felt

My insides

Imploding

But my lips

Had the audacity

To force a smile

And I

Appeared open

And I

Appeared approachable

And I

Hate that part of me

...The part that cancels my true feelings

As a rational response

Like there's

No

Rational

Explanation

For me

To react to pain

Like I don't deserve to

Like I don't really need to grieve

And if I do mourn

I need to measure the amount for sure

How awful it gets

When you can't even tell

If you're angry

Or just sad...

Or

If you asked for it

Or

You just forgot to tell him no with a little more certainty

MEASURABLE PAIN

In a world that only sees strength

I live in isolation

Applause for the triumph

And all that is conquered

Programming myself to be strong

Is the dagger in my heart

That people call a badge of honor

IN NEED OF
FORGIVENESS

Forgive me
If I don't want to be close
It's harmful to know
That I could love someone so much
Only to one day have to part

So forgive me
If I cannot accept love correctly
I am trying to find the worth in feelings
I am trying to understand
What it means to have them

Forgive me
If I isolate myself
I have a leak
Running out of my body
I don't want to spill my pain
On to you

Forgive me
Because my soul has an itching
And I worry
It will convince me
To project every fear and insecurity
Onto the ones I hold close

Please Forgive me
I am not who I once was
And I cannot be them again
Because who I was
Is made up
Of all
I have lost

THE
HOUSE
THAT
MADE

ME

I got news that my grandma passed

And it rained hard that night

Flooded...

Nothing was clear

I shed tears

On her dining room table

In the home

That had kept me stable

I used to light small fires

In that house

But just like the rain pouring down…

She would always put them out

And I don't need shelter from this storm

C A T C H

Hard being pretty
Say the privileged
How natural it is
For audiences to capture
The e s s e n c e
The *curve*
The CUT
Of your words

You are more than just a look
You have pretty girl abilities that you
Naturally developed
Because you believed
You were worth it

People validated you
Gave you the seal of approval
Easy money
Easy to count worth
When others can see it too

But honey
Girls like us
Got to pay a much higher price...
Just for a glimpse

I have to pat myself on the back
For feeling okay
With so many people
Not seeing me as
Worth the while

My make up
Whether it be genetic
Or cosmetic
Is not celebrated

2 2

Meaningless attractions
Empathy's been lacking
Nobody sees
Who I truly am
But they see glam

Empty encounters
I'm the prey
To the beasts
Of this evil world
Devoured
Then spat out
How pretty am I now?

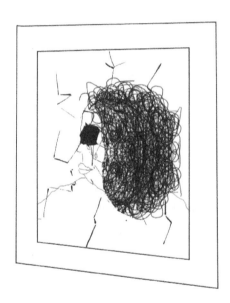

There are girls
Who want to punish me
Because they have never
Viewed themselves
As beautiful
But
View me as such

And what sucks is
What they don't know
What's been the problem
For me
Is that
I've felt the same before

WARS
WITH
SELF

When I was younger I believed life was magic

I wonder when it was that I first lost that sparkle in my eyes

When did my world turn grey?

Where did I misplace the joy I once had?

The child I was

Would have never dreamt of me

She would avoid this path

If she knew how damaged she'd be

The child I was

Is not the woman I am

I sometimes forget

ICE HEART

Used to flow free

Swish

And

Swash

And move

I would warm

And sometimes boil

But mostly, I'd be cool

With time I became still

      As I endured the brisk-hard-breeze

          Life was giving me cold weather

                I had no choice but to freeze

IN THE MOURNING

A terrible day it is
When daughters
Turn out to be the women
Their fathers never thought they *should* be

What a world crashing
Dream crushing day

The day
He finds
She's found
Her sexual presence

The day
She realizes
His love has limits because
He decides not to show her as much
And to care a little less

The day she finds
A purpose of her own

The day
She decides to settle in her own mind
And in her own ways

She will sit there
Alone
With her own
Addled
Over-cooked thoughts...

The sun will be vacant in her life
Even her moon will choose not to glow

What a terrible night it will be
To lose a love

But what a great love
She discovers for herself
In the *mourning*

WANDERLUST

Some people lose their way
      I never had one

An orphaned spirit
      Still searching for home

Settling at one place
      And then another
            As quickly as I can

Stuck deeply
      With inability
            To trust, just about anything

Walking in fear
      Waking with exhaustion

Too big and at times too little
      For the spaces I frequent often

I roam
With pitiful stories tucked under the caging of my chest

I roam
With sweet things inside that I want to give but I can't

I roam
With the hope that I'll find something worth stopping for

I roam for a chance to live…
For the freedom to exist

I roam
I roam
I roam
Until I find home

A PRAYER
IN THE DARK

If God can hear me, I don't know how I'm still where I am
I pray every day
I pray with my heart
I pray in my intent
I pray when I choose to do right
When my integrity outweighs my wins

Why am I losing...so much, so often?
I can't tell if I'm on the brink of a breakthrough
Or running circles inside of a curse
Am I cursed God?
Did you create me as example of what not to be?
A billboard of all the things you shouldn't seek?
Will my life be a tribute to pain?
Did you give me victory in my story?
Am I waiting on nothing?
I need this all to account for something

This is my heart praying, this is my intent speaking
This is me wanting to do right
This is my integrity
Giving one final play to overturn the game

L I G H T S   O U T

No wonder

This feels so close to death

No wonder it felt like they were burying me

Like the dirt was so heavy

Cause it was

It was so heavy that

It broke me

But I am not this shell

It broke me

And I am

Becoming something else

REST

It's lonely

In the cocoon

But

Good things

Happen in the dark, too

A CONVERSATION
WITH DESTINY

Could you tell me the time, please?

I can't tell when it is

I lost my mind somewhere down the road

And I was retracing my steps

I hope I'm not too late

Part Three:
Chasing Dawn
Moving Toward the light

When I first met you
I wondered
How our goodbye would go
It's no secret that everything *leaves*
Will you be back soon
My beautiful moon?

The moon: Do leaves come back to trees?

GROWING PAINS

Waking up to your worth
Is a process of pain
Your eyes slowly peel open
Your brain is rebooting
Bones creak
Body aches
You struggle to walk
Until you warm up
Until it loosens
And you feel
Like you are ready
To get what is yours

T O U G H   L O V E

It weighs on you
Cracks your back
Rearranges the bones in your body

It will crush
And suffocate
It will kneed the stiff out
Leaving you
Morphed, softened

This love
Will make you feel better
And you'll walk around at ease

BAD SEED

I'm not like those
Who are innately good
They don't seem to do any wrong
I'm not like those
Who see the reason
In why they do things a way
As who they naturally are

Because for me
It's been about
What you choose to fight against
I'm one of those bad seeds
Desperately holding on
To something good
Always fighting
For something good

SISTERS

Sisters can give us
The things
Our mothers misplaced
Or gave away
Or never had

They have
Given me
The brightest of light

Marking
A path
For me
To follow
Out of the dark

Thank God for her warmth

I SEE YOU IN RAINBOWS

I can't feel it

Until I do

Deep carvings

Against my once

Strong bones…

Numb

And then not

Focused

And then

Lost

You are

Dragging

Me through

A series of

Life altering narratives

Playing out in my head

I am wondering why

None of them

Involve not having you in the picture

I wonder why I am not dreaming

You are tied to me in ways I can't seem to understand

There are people in this world

That I need to know I made proud

Because the feeling of failing you

Sends me into

A cloud of darkness...

But thank God

For the rain they release

From my stinging eyes

Thank God

For the warmth of the day after the clouds pass

I thank God

That you found your way

And in some ways that sounds terrifying

But I need to believe

FAITHFUL THINKING

I don't know enough

About good times

So I'm leaning on

What could be

I'm banking on

Making it to better

And I'm hoping it's more

Than my mind has the capacity to imagine

WASHINGTON AVE.

I walked down many streets

I pass by them like they ain't mine

Cause they ain't

Where I'm from is where I'm at

But not where I'm gonna be

That's why

I'm walking down these streets

Passing by them like they ain't mine

...Someday they will be

But right now

Where I'm from

Is where I'm at

And that is all I have

Until I'm where I wanna be

OLD HABITS

Surely

I am certain

That I have no clue what's going on

And most of this shit is out of my hands

But

I am changing the ways

In which I handle things

My old pleasures

Are in the archive

INTROSPECTIVE

I could never make you love me
You'd have to decide that on your own

I cannot force you to be here
I'm fine with walking alone

I've been so busy these days
In my head
Looking for myself

Been so in tune with me
I don't see anyone else

THE SOUND OF FREEDOM

I like that part of me that gets fed up quick

That bitch I can turn into with a switch in my spit

I sense how it makes you feel

Something real

Maybe you ain't used to seeing

What your mind can't make up

Pardon me

If I pain the drum in your ear

Still, I need you to witness this

Doubters will apprehend

The inflection in my speech

My soul will be heard

By deaf souls

Who can't stand

The sound

Of my

Freedom

BEING A WOMXN
IS A
SERIOUS THING

Womxn

Wade   Where   Waters   Wait

Where   Wild   Was   Welcome

Where   We   Wet   Wombs

Where   Winners   Win

NO MORE MARTYRS

I'm so grounded
Roots deep
Loyal
The soil
Is every bit a part of me

But I ain't dying for the movement

I am
Growing up
And flowering
Towards the sun

That is keeping me alive

Some would rather
See me wither
And die

So
Best thing a seed could do
Is grow

Shift

Break

Do anything
But sit waiting
To be devoured
By pain
Bestowed upon you

What a precious gift it is...
Stand on it

Do not be crushed
And manipulated
Into thinking
Your life's
Purpose is made up
Of how much you can endure
Or
Assimilate

Your purpose
Is found in the seed that you are
So be it

The seed of a rose
Can be deemed
A mere
Seedling
All of its life
If it chooses
Not to grow

The seed of a rose
Will tell us
Who it is
By its blossom

Tell us...
Who you are
And maybe
We could all
Bloom
And not
Die
Seeds

WHEN
I GET
BACK
TO
BEING ME

When I get back to being me
I will do it selfishly
And I mean it

I won't have to dream it, Imma be it
Off the picture, off the wall, off the chain
Not a stain, getting change
Like Big Tuck said

Everyday living peace
And raising hell
My front door won't need a bell
Cause' home is in the shell
Of my mind
My frontal lobe is the only one of its kind

And with time
It all gets better
I'll be like what the hell
Was stormy weather?
Not much can ruffle these feathers
They have been grown anew

Who knew
I could shine this bright?
Mostly at night
The moon amongst a sea of dark
With scared dips all over me
Those are my trophies

And those who know me
Inspire me…
To give them more to know

I can only grow
There will be no emotions I'm afraid to show
My glow-up will finally glow
My teeth white as snow
XL
Super curly
Dipped out fro

INTERNAL AFFAIRS

It turns my stomach
Sometimes
How bad
How remedial life has been
Without you

How did it feel before
To not want this?
To never hope for it?

...Because ~~you were~~
You believed
You were
Damaged

And now
You made it a good thing

You make me want more for us
I am inspired by your story...

Am I falling in love with myself?

J O Y

I used to think

There was no depth

In the joy of solitude

Like it only sounds good

Or like the idea of it sounds nice

But you can

Actually

Experience joy when no one is watching

Joy...

That oversees

The false premises

That outside validation emits

RISE

Wake up

Wake up

Little butterfly

It's time for you to fly

Go

Be one with the sky

CALL ME MOTHER

My brain
Seems to
Float
And my heart beats gentle

I feel like
I can feel again

I've shed some pounds
In darkness
And self-loathing

I've shed some weight
In guilt

And in control
And in caring
Cause
Why should I?

Little parts of me
Are still babies
Still un-nurtured
Little
Infants

I can't make them carry themselves
I'm busy parenting

I don't have time for
Your bullshit

I have to grow myself up
I have protecting to do
I have to tend to the seeds
I just planted within myself

And they need time
Cause they weren't sown
All those years ago

So now that
I've uncovered
This rich
Unscathed soil
I'll make things grow

I'll cut down the poison
Infiltrating
My good roots
And destroying my homeland

NOTE TO SELF:
FOR THE MORNING

-How do you feel about yourself? Can you find the answer without an audience?

-When you start to doubt who you are, don't forget to ask why.

-Don't stop asking the hard questions.

-Be more concerned with being who you are, than showing who you are.

-Trust yourself to walk down the stairs without glancing at your feet.

-Your time is not bestowed to every person you meet.

-You practice loving yourself, because you never learned its pure form. Soul searching ain't nothing sweet.

-Give time to what you want to flourish.

-Fail with grace, Life is not a race.

-Remember your time with Grandma, remember to take up space.

-You have a lot to say. So no, there isn't any glory in hiding your face.

-Apologize to yourself.

-Create new meanings.

-Pray.

-And if you don't find yourself being the type of girl they want, Be the girl they can't have.

-When you're vibrating low, Acknowledge it.

-Embrace The unknown.

-Care about your space.

-Pace yourself.
-Sometimes people don't understand what they don't want to,
-So don't force them to understand you.
-You are worth so much more than you give credit to.
-what's constant about you, can only lie within you.
-Learn to disband.
-You don't have to worry about liking every part of who you are, You won't.
But you do deserve love.
-Make life happen for you.
-Be moving.
-Stay loose.

You have the right
To have a world full of problems
And still feel light.
And still feel happy.

Don't let this world make you forget yourself.
And don't you regret any piece of it.

-Asia

Girls like us sometimes love ourselves in parts,
At a time, on the way to wholeness.

About the Author

Asia Upton was born in 1994 in Kansas City, Kansas. Asia is a published writer and poet. Her love for words has always been deeply rooted in her innate ability to express herself artistically. She was involved in her high school newspaper and yearbook which led to her studies in Journalism at Kansas State University. Having published works in the Royal Purple, The Collegian and a poem in Jenifer Fennell's *Keep Living* journal, *A Night With Me* is Asia's first book.

To read more visit www.poetichumm.com

Made in the USA
Monee, IL
08 January 2024

50320544R00049